10 S

Success

An Exercise in Career

Tim Marvel

10SecondsDaily.com

10 Seconds   A Daily Exercise

© 2015 Tim Marvel. All rights reserved. No part of the publication may be reproduced, distributed, or transmitted in any form or by any means, including photocopying, recording, or other electronic or mechanical methods, without the prior written permission of the publisher, except in the case of brief quotations embodied in critical reviews and certain other noncommercial uses permitted by copyright law.

10 Seconds   A Daily Exercise

This book is dedicated to my wife, Rockie, the love of my life. Thank you for being my inspiration.

And to God for giving me the gift of encouragement. May I always use that gift to bless You.

Acknowledgments

I want to thank my team. You amazing people help bring my ideas to life and I'm grateful for your insights.

My wife, Rockie.
My mother and lifetime supporter, Nancy Cabana.
My business consultant, Susan Hamilton.
My graphic artist, Mai Koua.
My editor, Lori Freeland.

Introduction

DO you see professional success as the result of random luck you just can't find? A giant leap you need to make right now? Something that requires a confidence you know you'll never have?

I did.

It took me years to realize two crucial truths. I had to learn to be happy where I was before I could move forward. And I needed a written career timeline of concrete goals, both short and long term, that I treated as a plan of action.

Don't stay stuck. Dream big. Adjust your goals as different opportunities present themselves. And don't see failure as a stop sign. See it as a way to refine your goals.

Be the best "you" you can be right now. Then use that to carry yourself forward. Meeting each small goal, step by step, takes you to the finish line.

My Story

NO matter job title, salary, or kudos given, everyone has some insecurity when it comes to their career. I managed to hide mine for a long time. Mostly because up until a certain point I'd always been at least mildly successful, despite the fact I didn't have an easy start.

Immediately following high school graduation, I married and soon after had a baby on the way, leaving no time and no dollars to put toward a college education. Four years of service in the navy solved the immediate need for insurance and a steady paycheck, but living on a submarine wasn't what I wanted to do forever.

Once my tour ended, I accepted a job in retail and discovered I was good at sales. Yet, each time I'd reach a certain level of promotion, I'd be told that without that college degree I wouldn't go far.

Insecurities popped up, but I ignored them and looked for other career options. Through a friend's suggestion, I took a sales job at a car dealership. And did phenomenally well. Right away, I earned the title *Thirty*

Car Guy—which meant I sold thirty cars in a month. In addition, six months out of twelve, I made top salesperson.

The instant success went straight to my attitude, the money I made settled me in, and what was supposed to be a temporary fix turned into a permanent position. In the back of my mind, I stuck my nose up at those retail stores. I was doing great. And without a college education.

In my late twenties, my mother needed my help. I could sell cars anywhere, so I moved from Virginia Beach to a dealership in Texas. Once there, promotions came quickly. I went from Salesperson to Finance Manager to Sales Manager. My fast-track career continued to inflate my already enlarged ego and my arrogant attitude spilled over into my personal life.

As I was being groomed to make General Sales Manager, the organization that owned my dealership sold to another organization. They moved me to another store where I continued toward my next step promotion.

Soon after I changed locations, my previous General Manager convinced me to come to his new store. I was doing well where I was, but the offer was a big deal—five new car franchises and three used car departments.

Considering I'd started my career being told I'd get nowhere without a college education, the money and instant promotion offered were more than my overinflated ego could resist.

I took over the sales department and the store gained market share, profits rose, and the previously poor customer satisfaction greatly improved. I had arrived. And I was feeling pretty great about it.

One morning, nine months into my dream job, I walked into the office to find my General Manager—the guy that came after me to come work with him—standing by my desk with a sick look on his face. He wouldn't look me in the eye. "Keep your demo car until you find another gig." He handed me a white envelope. "There's a couple month's pay to hold you over."

It took me more than a few heart-stopping moments to realize I'd just been fired.

My pride hit the floor, my ego crashing hard like the monstrosity it was. Shock, embarrassment, betrayal, devastation, and fear tore up my gut. What had I done wrong? Everything I'd worked years for was gone in less than a minute. All the insecurities I'd pushed down since

I'd left retail rushed back. I got fired because I'd never deserved that job. I hadn't been equipped, educated, or professional enough.

I had to have a job. I'd always had a job. I couldn't *not* work. Never in my life had I felt so lost and alone, with absolutely no idea what to do next. The panic churning inside me wasn't so much about losing the money as it was about losing my identity. Desperate, I made some calls on my way home and set up whatever interviews I could find.

Since my lofty goals of being General Sales Manager were dust and I was clearly an ultimate loser when it came to my career, I took a job that didn't challenge me. I became the sales manager at a smaller dealership. My thought was—at least my job would be safe. But within a short period of time, the manager I replaced moved back. Once again, I was about to be fired.

My insecurities resurfaced again. Worse this time. Losing two jobs in a row? Had to be my fault. Professionally, I was worthless.

Because I didn't want to move again, I asked the owner of the dealership to let me step down to being a salesman. Based on my record as a good employee, he agreed to let me keep my current title, to fill in as a floating manager here and there, and we came to a fair compensation. But not without my pride feeling severely stepped on. The next day I stepped out onto the sales floor to sell cars—something I hadn't done in years.

Because sales came naturally to me, my ego began to heal. I changed my perspective and my attitude. Maybe I could be happy back in sales. Maybe being on the floor would help me understand where and if I'd gone wrong in training my sales staff over the years. Or at least help me figure out why I'd been fired.

The attitude change was a good thing. But I stopped there and didn't take the next step toward the career I wanted. A paralyzing fear of failure remained, telling me if I tried to make a vertical move again, I'd crash and burn.

Fear of making a mistake kept me on the sales floor ten more years. It took a cycling accident to shake me up and a wedding to the woman of my dreams to give me confidence to make some tough decisions and realize it was time to find the confidence to walk out of my comfort zone.

Being General Sales Manager did not end up being my end destination. I ultimately found my joy in training others. But that's another story. While I wish I wouldn't have let that painful episode of getting fired keep me down for so long, I'm grateful I finally decided to start taking the baby steps that landed me where I am today.

I've accomplished more in my career than I ever thought was possible. But not without running into challenges and failures along the way. Over the years, I've learned that achieving true success and meeting my goals is all about pushing through those challenges and finding ways to make my failures work *for* me rather than *against* me.

I've learned failure isn't the end of the line. It's the road to a new beginning.

Your Story

PROFESSIONAL success doesn't have to be defined by hefty promotions or substantial job changes. And sometimes the path you're on isn't the one that will drop you at your ultimate destination.

No matter where you're at or where you want to go, success is about attitude—how you perceive yourself as a professional—and setting and meeting your career goals.

For years, I viewed my professional success as accidental and my failure as the same. I didn't ever really feel a sense of control when it came to work. But hindsight is a gift. Looking back, I realize my success or failure directly tied to the things I believed about myself and the small tasks I did or did not accomplish daily.

We're all unique individuals and we figure life out in different ways. To keep going, some of us need encouragement in the form of kind words and a pat on the back. Others of us need to crash into a deep ravine to realize we need to make a change. One thing we all need to do is set goals. It's hard to move forward if we don't know where we're heading.

Here's how *10 Seconds Success* works. In the morning, read the thought or challenge for the day. Watch for ways to implement the idea. In the evening, make notes about what you learned. Be real. Ask yourself hard questions. Challenge your answers.

You get out of something what you put into it. The honesty is for you.

As you go through your thirty day journey, take time to discover what helps you get organized, motivates you during your work day, and gets you excited about moving forward in your career. Then put into place the daily disciplines. If you're consistent, making tiny ten-second tweaks can carry the power to set you apart professionally.

Good luck! I'm rooting for you to be amazed at what you discover about yourself.

Day 1

Morning:

How you define professional success? Piece together your definition as you walk through your business day.

Evening:

Picture yourself successful. Write down what that looks likes. Consider not only what you want out of your career, but who you want to be as a person.

_____
_____
_____
_____
_____
_____
_____
_____

10 Seconds   A Daily Exercise

Day 2

Morning:

Where are you in your career timeline? Think about your professional goals today.

Evening:

What did you discover about where you're standing now compared to where you'd like to go? Draw yourself a timeline of your professional goals, both short term and long term. Don't be afraid to dream big.

_____
_____
_____
_____
_____
_____
_____

Day 3

Morning:

Most people don't realize how much attitude fuels their success. Pay attention to your attitude.

Evening:

Rate your attitude at work today. 1 being negative. 10 being positive. Also note how your attitude changed as you handled various tasks.

_____

_____

_____

_____

_____

_____

_____

_____

Day 4

Morning:

Successful people feel satisfied. Satisfaction stems from a positive attitude. Think about adjusting your attitude as a way to redefine your success.

Evening:

How can changing your attitude redefine your career goals and how you'll reach them? Tweak your goal timeline if necessary.

___
___
___
___
___
___
___
___

Day 5

Morning:

Watch for what helps or hinders you in relation to your career goals. Job limitations? Education? Fear? Attitude? Co-workers? Supervisors?

Evening:

List obstacles that hold you back and ways to overcome them.

_____
_____
_____
_____
_____
_____
_____
_____

10 Seconds A Daily Exercise

Day 6

Morning:

When it comes to completing your timeline of career goals, do you have all the knowledge and resources you need?

Evening:

Make a note of a book to investigate, a class to take, or a person to reach out to.

_____

_____

_____

_____

_____

_____

_____

Day 7

Morning:

Find a mentor. Be a mentor. Look around for people you need to include in your life.

Evening:

People give to those they see giving. It's that old adage, "You reap what you sow." Sow big. List a few people you can help. Then list a few people you can ask for help.

_____

_____

_____

_____

_____

_____

_____

_____

Day 8

Morning:

Tiny tweaks build the foundation for success. Look for things you have the power to change.

Evening:

What small things did you find to tweak? Commit to search for ways to make small adjustments every day, even if they're only internal.

_____

_____

_____

_____

_____

_____

_____

_____

Day 9

Morning:

You've listed your goals and defined success. Think about ways to measure your progress.

Evening:

Write a plan of action in regard to your short and long term goals. Remember, accomplishing smaller goals pushes you toward your bigger goals.

_____

_____

_____

_____

_____

_____

_____

_____

Day 10

Morning:

Do you struggle to achieve goals? Remind yourself of something hard you completed in the past.

Evening:

How did it feel to finish a difficult task? Apply that feeling forward. List rewards you can give yourself for meeting goals on your career path.

_____

_____

_____

_____

_____

_____

_____

_____

Day 11

Morning:

Be aware of useless tasks that take your time and energy.

Evening:

List a task or two you can eliminate from your daily routine. Maybe it's something you can quit doing or something you can delegate.

_____
_____
_____
_____
_____
_____
_____
_____

Day 12

Morning:

We do a few things well or a lot of things poorly. Think about the tasks you need to complete today. Than pick the top three. Make them a priority for your time and energy.

Evening:

What happened when you prioritized your list of tasks? How can you extend that into a daily occurrence?

_____
_____
_____
_____
_____
_____
_____
_____

Day 13

Morning:

Who holds you accountable when it comes to your career? Think beyond your boss's demands to people who will encourage you as you walk your path.

Evening:

List people who will ask hard questions and push you to move forward, especially when you get discouraged or complacent. Then ask them to help you achieve your goals.

_____

_____

_____

_____

_____

_____

_____

_____

Day 14

Morning:

Work on your inner professionalism today. When you walk out the door, are you mentally prepared to conquer your day? Is work foremost on your mind?

Evening:

List ways to be more prepared tomorrow. Do you need to boost your confidence? Do you need to spend more time getting pumped to face your business day?

_____

_____

_____

_____

_____

_____

_____

_____

Day 15

Morning:

Repeating a daily positive affirmation settles your mind and improves your attitude. Try it. Say something right now that gives you what you need to face the day.

Evening:

Make a list of positive affirmations. Think about what you struggle with and go from there.

_____
_____
_____
_____
_____
_____
_____

Day 16

Morning:

Enthusiasm breeds enthusiasm. Test that theory. Go to work excited to be there.

Evening:

Rate your level of enthusiasm at work on a scale of 1-10. How did others respond to you when you showed up excited about work?

Day 17

Morning:

Begin to look outward. Study yourself in the mirror. Do you see someone you would do business with today?

Evening:

Create a mental image of the professional you want to be—clean, well-dressed, approachable—and commit that image to memory. Work on creating that person daily.

_____

_____

_____

_____

_____

_____

_____

Day 18

Morning:

Dressing professionally boosts confidence. Watch for how your choice of wardrobe affects your attitude, the way you interact with others, and the way others respond to you.

Evening:

What does what you wear say about you as a professional? Can you change some small things? Iron your clothes. Buy a new suit. Try out some new shoes.

Day 19

Morning:

Ask yourself how your coworkers and/or clients perceive you today.

Evening:

Think about impressions. How important are they? How can you project your best self every day, both internally and externally?

_____
_____
_____
_____
_____
_____
_____
_____

Day 20

Morning:

Go to work and imagine yourself on *Candid Camera*. Walk through a typical day and "record" what happens.

Evening:

As you watch your replay, rate your professionalism on a scale of 1-10. How did you do? Where do you need to put in some effort?

Day 21

Morning:

There's a balance between "slacker" and "workaholic." Where do you fall on an average work day?

Evening:

How many hours a week do you work? Too few? Too many? Where can you make adjustments? Don't forget to factor in rest as you run after your goals.

Day 22

Morning:

Watch for what concerns you at work. What trips you up? What keeps you locked where you are in your career?

Evening:

Outline your concerns. Are they concrete or only in your head? List an action plan to move past them.

_____

_____

_____

_____

_____

_____

_____

Day 23

Morning:

Making decisions eliminates clutter in your mind. Look for decisions that need to be made and clear them out.

Evening:

What opportunities have you been ignoring that you need to commit to one way or the other? Tie up those loose ends and move on.

_____
_____
_____
_____
_____
_____
_____
_____

Day 24

Morning:

Mastering little things at work leads to mastering larger things.

Evening:

What little things did you master today? What can you add tomorrow?

_____

_____

_____

_____

_____

_____

_____

_____

Day 25

Morning:

Know in advance, do in advance. Today, watch for things you could've planned and been more prepared to handle.

Evening:

What did you discover? List one task you can complete for tomorrow to get ahead of your day.

_____

_____

_____

_____

_____

_____

_____

_____

Day 26

Morning:

Success sometimes requires sacrifice. Watch for things you can give up today.

Evening:

Did you find anything to sacrifice that will help you move forward with your career goals? TV time? Social Media? Long lunches out of the office? Co-workers that deflate you rather than inflate you?

Day 27

Morning:

Today, leave your comfort zone at home. As you walk toward your career goals, challenge yourself to take a bigger step today. Even if that step feels scary.

Evening:

List ways you challenge or motivate yourself to do more. Competition? Rewards? Affirmations? Are there new ways you can list that might work better?

Day 28

Morning:

Are you a competitive person? Does that character trait extend to work? Be on the lookout for an answer today.

Evening:

Does competition push you forward or hold you back? List ways to adjust your attitude accordingly.

_____

_____

_____

_____

_____

_____

_____

_____

Day 29

Morning:

Persistence and consistence are important disciplines to possess. Ask yourself if you have them today.

Evening:

Are you consistent with your efforts? Do you persist in times of trial? If not, commit to changing that today.

Day 30

Morning:

Today when you go to work, remind yourself where you were five, ten, or fifteen years ago.

Evening:

Always remember where you started. Take a trip down memory lane and list the goals you've already accomplished. You might amaze yourself.

_____
_____
_____
_____
_____
_____
_____

10 Seconds   A Daily Exercise

Notes:_____

Conclusion

OVER the last thirty days, I hope you've discovered you don't have to be stuck in your career.

It doesn't matter where you're starting or how many mistakes you've made in the past, you can achieve your professional goals. You just have to keep walking forward.

Investment managers advise you to pay yourself first. Apply that advice toward your career and create a plan to continue what you've started.

There are 86,400 seconds in a day. Take *10 Seconds* to invest in yourself. You've worked hard. Don't stop now.

I've developed the following questions to help guide your journey.

The Plan

1. Where am I in my career now? This is your baseline to measure change.

2. Where do I want to be in the next month, year, five years? These are your short term and long term goals.

3. What steps are you willing to take to reach those goals? This is your plan of action.

4. Who knows about your desire to change? It's difficult to police yourself. This is your accountability.

Top Ten Quick Business Tips

1. Make Lists.
2. Be prepared for your day, your week, your month.
3. Search and destroy distractions.
4. Commit to complete tasks on time.
5. Compete against yourself, not others.
6. If your way isn't working, change what you're doing.
7. Be on time.
8. Acknowledge others around you.
9. Never assume you know what another person is thinking. Ask.
10. Treat everyone with respect.

Do you struggle with your attitude?

10 Seconds: An Exercise in Attitude is available now.

Are you tired of feeling defeated before you even start your day?

Between the headlines, social media, and the people around us, we have the potential to be filled with negative input from the moment we wake up to the moment we go to bed. Even while we sleep, we continue to process what we've absorbed.

We become what we believe.

If we live in constant negativity, it's no wonder we struggle to be positive. We may not be able to fix all our problems, but we can change the way we respond.

Our attitude influences our perception. Our perception becomes our reality.

What would happen if we took ten seconds to plant a positive seed in our attitude each morning? Over time, those tiny seeds can shift our perception and help us cultivate a new reality.

Self-reflection is the front line for change.

Take back your life in *10 Seconds* a day.

Meeting goals isn't about grand leaps.

It's about persistent steps and tiny tweaks.

Commit to continue

"The 10 Second Challenge."

Your next ten seconds begin now.

How far will you go?

Visit **10SecondsDaily.com**

for additional resources including daily blogs, videos, workbooks, events, and to invite Tim to come to your organization and speak.

Printed in Germany
by Amazon Distribution
GmbH, Leipzig